Garrett Morgan

Inventor of the Traffic Light and Gas Mask

Patricia J. Murphy

Enslow Publishers, Inc.

40 Industrial Road   PO Box 38
Box 398   Aldershot
Berkeley Heights, NJ 07922   Hants GU12 6BP
USA   UK

http://www.enslow.com

I would like to thank the following people for assistance with this biography:
Sandra Morgan, Garrett Morgan's granddaughter and family spokesperson; and the Federal Highway
Adminstration's staff, who made my interview with Ms. Morgan possible.
Thank you!   —P.J.M.

Library of Congress Cataloging-in-Publication Data

Murphy, Patricia J., 1963–
    Garrett Morgan : inventor of the traffic light and gas mask / Patricia J. Murphy.
        p. cm. — (Famous inventors)
    ISBN 0-7660-2274-9 (hardcover)
    1. Traffic signs and signals—Juvenile literature. 2. Gas masks—Juvenile literature. 3. African American
inventors—Biography—Juvenile literature. 4. Morgan, Garrett A., 1877–1963—Juvenile literature.
    [1. Morgan, Garrett A., 1877–1963. 2. Inventors. 3. African Americans—Biography.] I. Title. II. Series.
    TE228.M87 2004
    609.2—dc22

                                                                                                                2003026954

Printed in the United States of America

10 9 8 7 6 5 4 3 2 1

To Our Readers:
We have done our best to make sure all Internet Addresses in this book were active and appropriate when we
went to press. However, the author and the publisher have no control over and assume no liability for the material available on those Internet sites or on other Web sites they may link to. Any comments or suggestions can
be sent by e-mail to comments@enslow.com or to the address on the back cover.

Every effort has been made to locate all copyright holders of material used in this book. If any errors or omis-
sions have occurred, corrections will be made in future editions of this book.

Illustration Credits: The Cleveland Press Collection, Cleveland State University Library, pp. 3, 6L, 15, 28, 29B;
Enslow Publishers, Inc., p. 16; Hemera Technologies, Inc., p. 23; Library of Congress, pp. 7, 8, 10, 11, 20, 25;
photo courtesy of Diana Rogers, pp. 1, 2, 29T; U.S. Patent Office, pp. 17, 22; The Western Reserve Historical
Society, Cleveland, Ohio, pp. 4, 6R, 12, 13, 18, 19, 26, 27.

Cover Illustration: The Western Reserve Historical Society, Cleveland, Ohio (portrait, medal); photo courtesy of
Diana Rogers (traffic light); U.S. Patent Office (drawing).

Table of Contents

Garrett Augustus Morgan

Chapter 1

Looking for Work

Garrett Morgan, age thirty-nine, ran out of the house in his pajamas. It was the middle of the night, July 25, 1916. An explosion had trapped workers digging a tunnel under Lake Erie in Ohio. They needed one of Garrett's inventions—and fast.

Garrett and his brother Frank dashed to the tunnel. They brought along some of Garrett's "safety hoods." Garrett, Frank, and two others put them on.

When some workers were trapped in a tunnel, Garrett and his safety hoods saved the day.

The hoods covered their faces and had long tubes to reach the air near the ground. That air was fresher. Garrett and the others crawled through dust, gas, and smoke to pull out the trapped workers. For some of the men it was too late, but others were saved.

Garrett Augustus Morgan was born on March 4, 1877. He was the seventh of eleven children. His parents, Sydney and Elizabeth Reed Morgan, had once been slaves, but now they were free. Garrett's father worked on the railroad. His mother took care of the family.

Young Garrett grew up in Paris, Kentucky. The part of town where he lived was called Claysville. People there were African American and poor. They worked on farms or on the railroad. Like most children in Claysville, Garrett left school after

When Garrett was a boy in Kentucky, most of the people he knew worked on farms.

fifth grade. It was time for him to earn some money. Garrett did not want to be a farmer or to work on the railroad. At age fourteen, he went to Cincinnati, Ohio, to find a different kind of job.

Soon Garrett found work as a handyman on a rich man's farm. He wanted to be able to read and write better, so he hired someone to teach him.

In 1895, when he was eighteen, Garrett moved to Cleveland, Ohio. There he found work sweeping floors and doing odd jobs at a large clothing factory called Roots & McBride. This job would change Garrett's life.

Garrett started working in a factory in Cleveland.

Chapter 2

Getting Into Business

Even as a young boy, Garrett had been interested in machines and how they work. At the clothing factory, Garrett saw that the belts that helped run the sewing machines snapped all the time. Garrett had an idea about how to make a better sewing machine belt. He made one and showed it to the factory owners. They paid Garrett $150 for his invention. Then they gave him a job fixing sewing machines.

Garrett had married a woman named Madge Nelson in 1896, but they divorced after only two years. Now he began spending time with Mary Anne Hasek, a seamstress at the factory.

News of Garrett's talent with machines spread through Cleveland. He started fixing sewing machines at other clothing factories, too. By 1907 Garrett had saved enough money to buy a home. He also opened a shop for selling and fixing sewing machines. In 1908 he married Mary Anne. Over the years they had three sons, John Pierpoint, Garrett Jr., and Cosmos Henry.

A woman who does sewing as her job is called a seamstress.

Garrett wanted to make sewing machines
work even better.

Garrett liked being a businessman, and he was good at it. In 1909 he opened up a tailor shop. He hired thirty-two workers to sew fancy coats, dresses, suits, and children's clothing. In another business he sold poultry—chickens, turkeys, ducks, and geese.

Garrett was very busy, but he still found time to work on new inventions. With each invention, Garrett fixed a problem. His hat fastener kept hats from flying off women's heads. He had many ideas to make sewing machines work better, too.

Like many other inventors, Garrett made one of his discoveries by accident. He wanted to solve a problem with sewing machine needles. They moved so quickly that they got too hot. Sometimes they left burn marks on the cloth. Could Garrett make the needles slide up and down easier?

He coated a needle with a mixture of chemicals. Then he wiped his hands off on a fuzzy piece of cloth. A little later, the fuzzy bits of cloth were sticking out straight. What was going on?

Garrett tried some of his mixture on a friend's dog and on his own head. The dog's fur and Garrett's hair became straight! Garrett had invented

Garrett and two of his sons.

Garrett, right, invented and sold many hair products.

a product to straighten hair. He called it Garrett A. Morgan Hair Refining Cream. Then he started a company to make and sell this cream and other hair care products. Many people bought hair care products from Garrett. His business was a big success.

Chapter 3

Garrett's "Safety Hood"

arrett's next invention was very important. He knew that smoke and poison gases were a deadly problem for firefighters. Garrett wanted to invent a hood to protect firefighters by helping them breathe clean air.

Garrett and his brother Frank studied fires, smoke, and chemical gases. In a fire, the smoke rises. The air closest to the floor is safer to breathe.

One day Garrett was at the circus. He saw an elephant stick its trunk outside the circus tent to suck fresh air.

The elephant's trunk was like a long tube. So Garrett made his safety hoods with long tubes. Then the firefighters could breathe the cleaner air near the ground.

Garrett tested his invention in different kinds of fires. He wore the hood for twenty minutes in a tent filled with thick smoke from burning chemicals. It worked! In 1914, the hood won the top prize at a show of new safety products in New York City.

Garrett got an idea at the circus.

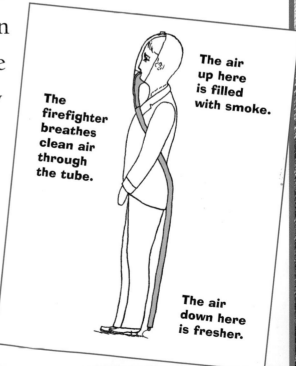

The air up here is filled with smoke.

The firefighter breathes clean air through the tube.

The air down here is fresher.

Fire wagons in 1900 looked very different from today's fire trucks.

Garrett asked the United States government to give him a patent for his safety hood. This is a paper that says the inventor of an idea is the only person allowed to make and sell it. In 1915, Garrett was given the patent. He started a company to make Morgan Safety Hoods.

A year later, Garrett's safety hoods were used to save the workers trapped under Lake Erie. Garrett was a hero, and his Morgan Safety Hoods became famous. Firefighters all over the country wanted to buy them.

Garrett got a patent for his safety hood.

Garrett traveled from state to state to show his safety hoods. Sometimes he ran into problems when people learned that he was African American. At that time, African Americans were not treated fairly. White and black people could not live together, go to school together, or work together.

Some people decided not to buy Garrett's safety hood because he was African American. Garrett knew this was wrong, but never let it stop him.

Garrett's safety hood could protect workers when they used power tools.

Garrett traveled all over to sell his safety hoods to firefighters in other states.

Garrett kept thinking of changes to make his hood even better. Later, the United States government made a gas mask using Garrett's ideas. These masks would protect soldiers from poison gases during war.

Cars and horses jammed the city streets.
There were many accidents.

Chapter 4

The Traffic Safety System

 ne day in 1922, a car and a horse-drawn carriage crashed into each other at a busy street corner. Garrett saw it happen. He was very upset.

The city streets were crowded with people, horse-drawn carriages, and cars. There were some traffic signals with STOP and GO signs, but they did not do much good. People and drivers had no warning when traffic would stop in one direction or go in the other.

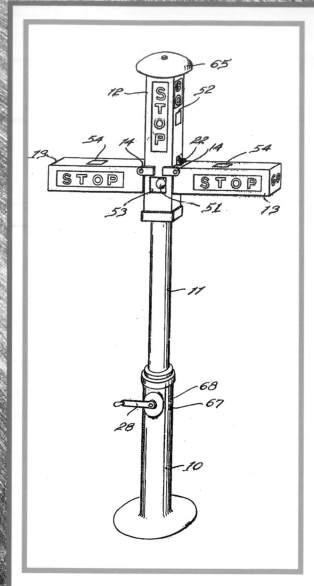

With his traffic signal, Garrett hoped the streets would be safer.

Garrett made pictures of his ideas for a traffic signal. He drew a pole with lights and folding arms that said STOP and GO. After many experiments, Garrett invented the Garrett A. Morgan Safety System. This traffic signal was used for many years. It was the model for today's red-yellow-green traffic lights.

A policeman stood next to Garrett's traffic signal to pull the arms up and down. When STOP and GO were halfway down, it meant cars should slow down because the signal was about to change. If the STOP arms were down, all traffic had to stop so that people could walk across the street.

Garrett started the Garrett Morgan National Safety Company to sell his traffic signals. In 1923, the government gave him a patent for his idea. That same year, the General Electric Company paid Garrett $40,000 to buy his patent. Then General Electric could make and sell the traffic signals.

Traffic signals were placed at a few busy streets in Cleveland. Soon other towns heard about them and wanted to buy some. After a while, other countries began using Garrett's ideas, too.

Today's traffic lights use Garrett's ideas.

Garrett became a rich man. He used some of the money to buy a large farm near Wakeman, Ohio.

Chapter 5

Working for Equal Rights

Garrett wanted to make life better for all people. He never forgot what it was like to be poor. He knew how it felt to be treated unfairly because of the color of his skin. All his life, Garrett worked for equal rights for African Americans. He believed that everyone should be able to have a good job, live in a nice home, and follow his or her dreams.

Garrett was one of the first members of the

Cleveland Association of Colored People. This group was started to help the African Americans in Cleveland gain equal rights under the law. It later became part of the National Association for the Advancement of Colored People (NAACP). Garrett also donated money and worked with other groups that helped people in need.

In the 1920s, Garrett began publishing the

Garrett gave his time and money to help the NAACP. This group was working hard to change unfair laws.

Cleveland Call newspaper. It was one of the first newspapers for African Americans. In 1931, he ran for the city council in Cleveland. He hoped to be a strong voice for the rights of African Americans in Cleveland. Garrett lost the election, but people heard his important speeches about civil rights.

In his later years, Garrett never stopped making inventions. He was becoming blind from an eye disease, but that did not stop his busy mind from playing with new ideas. He invented an electric hair-curling comb, and safety pellets for ashtrays. The pellets put out cigarettes that people left burning. Garrett lived long enough to enjoy a special exhibit in Chicago in 1963 that showed many of his inventions.

Garrett won many awards and honors for his inventions.

Garrett died on July 27, 1963. He was eighty-six years old. Many people have praised Garrett's life and work. Today, he is best remembered for inventing the first gas mask and the first traffic signal.

Garrett did not start out with money or education. Yet he did so much with his life. He never stopped working or thinking of new ideas. Garrett often told his children and his grandchildren, "Work with your head!" With his inventions, Garrett Morgan helped to make the world we live in a safer place.

In his newspaper, Garrett published articles of interest to African Americans in Cleveland.

Garrett's busy mind was always thinking
of new ideas and inventions.

Timeline

1877~Born March 4 in Claysville, Kentucky.

1891~Goes to Cincinnati to find work.

1895~Moves to Cleveland and works in a sewing machine factory.

1907~Opens sewing machine sales and repair shop.

1908~Marries Mary Anne Hasek.

1909~Starts tailoring and poultry businesses.

1914~Receives a patent for his "Safety Hood."

1920~Starts the *Cleveland Call* newspaper.

1923~Receives a patent for his "Safety System."

1931~Runs for city council, but loses the election.

1960s~Invents electric curling iron and smoking pellets.

1963~Dies July 27 in Cleveland, Ohio.

city council—The group of people who are elected to run the government of a city.

National Association for the Advancement of Colored People (NAACP)—A group started to help all Americans gain equal rights under the law. The NAACP is one of the oldest civil rights organizations in the United States.

patent—A government paper that states who is allowed to make and sell a new invention.

seamstress—A woman whose job is sewing.

slave—A person who is owned by another person and must work without being paid.

tailor—Someone whose job is to sew clothing for other people.

Learn More

Books

Hudson, Wade. *Five Notable Inventors.* New York: Scholastic, 1995.

Sullivan, Otha Richard. *Black Stars: African-American Inventors.* New York: John Wiley and Sons, 1998.

Video

The Garrett Augustus Morgan Story. Kansas City, Mo.: Video Gems MT Productions, 1996.

Internet Addresses

Garrett Morgan
 <http://www.si.edu/lemelson/centerpieces/iap/inventors_morg.html>

The Inventions of Garrett Morgan
 <http://www.sciencemuseum.org.uk/on-line/garret-morgan/index.asp>

Index